better together*

* This book is best read together, grownup and kid.

akidsco.com

a
kids
book
about

a
kids
book
about
ONLINE
SAFETY

by OIC Security Group

A Kids Co.
Editor Emma Wolf
Designer Rick DeLucco
Creative Director Rick DeLucco
Studio Manager Kenya Feldes
Sales Director Melanie Wilkins
Head of Books Jennifer Goldstein
CEO and Founder Jelani Memory

DK
Senior Production Editor Jennifer Murray
Senior Production Controller Louise Minihane
Senior Acquisitions Editor Katy Flint
Acquisitions Project Editor Sara Forster
Managing Art Editor Vicky Short
Managing Director, Licensing Mark Searle

First American edition, 2025
Published in the United States by DK Publishing, 1745 Broadway, 20th Floor,
New York, NY 10019

First published in Great Britain in 2025 by
Dorling Kindersley Limited, 20 Vauxhall Bridge Road, London SW1V 2SA
A Penguin Random House Company

The authorised representative in the EEA is
Dorling Kindersley Verlag GmbH. Arnulfstr. 124, 80636 Munich, Germany

A catalog record for this book is available from the Library of Congress.
A CIP catalogue record for this book is available from the British Library.
ISBN: 978-0-2417-4315-7

DK books are available at special discounts when purchased in bulk for sales
promotions, premiums, fund-raising, or education use. For details, contact:
DK Publishing Special Markets, 1745 Broadway, 20th Floor, New York, NY 10019
SpecialSales@dk.com

Printed and bound in China
www.dk.com
akidsco.com

To kids online everywhere, who remind us every day why we do what we do to keep them safe.

Intro
for grownups

The Internet has become an integral part of our lives. It offers a wealth of information, connection, and entertainment. However, with this vast digital landscape comes potential dangers, like bad actors lying about who they are and intending harm for their own gain. They may want to steal personal information, money, or even people.

What do you currently know about online safety, and what precautions do you already take?

This book aims to equip kids with essential online safety skills and empower grownups to have meaningful conversations about navigating the web wisely. Learn how you can keep the Internet both safe and fun!

>>>>> We are a group of online safety and security professionals.

Our jobs are to keep people safe online—people just like you!

You might be wondering
what online safety is.

THAT'S WHAT THIS BOOK IS ALL ABOUT!

Online safety means keeping
you and your information
safe when you are online.*

*Being online means using apps, games, or other tools
that connect you to other people through the Internet.

This looks like being careful about what you share on the Internet, and being cautious about people or websites you interact with.

Make no mistake,

THE INTERNET
AMAZING

PLACE!

You can play games,
watch videos, learn new things,
and talk to your friends.

You can also be anyone
you want to be—
you can pretend to be

a pirate,

or a musician,

or even a wizard.

But some people pretend to be someone else in order to hurt others.

They may pretend to like you to gain your trust and then convince you to do something unsafe.

They may pretend to be someone they are not in order to take something from you.

They may lie to you, or trick you into giving away your personal information.*

*Personal information includes your phone number, email address, usernames, passwords, real name, where you live, where you go to school, or pictures of you and your family.

That sounds pretty serious, doesn't it?

But what does it mean?

WELL, LET US TELL

YOU A STORY. >>>>>>

MEET

JIMMY!

He loves playing online games with his friends.

One day, Jimmy began playing
with some new people he met online.

Not only did they also love gaming, but they told Jimmy they were the same age and went to a school nearby.

After playing online together for a few weeks, one of Jimmy's new friends, Adam, asked Jimmy to send him some pictures of himself.

WHAT SHOULD JIMMY DO NEXT?

WHAT WOULD YOU DO?

Jimmy told his grownups
about Adam asking for pictures.

(THIS IS THE RIG

HT THING TO DO!)

Jimmy and his grownups decided that Jimmy should ask anytime he wants to send pictures to someone online, and that he wouldn't send pictures to Adam.

HIS PARENTS WERE
CONCERNED BY ADAM'S
REQUEST, AND BECAUSE
THEY HAD NEVER MET ADAM.

WE THINK
JIMMY AND
HIS GROWNUPS
HANDLED THIS
PERFECTLY.

Jimmy told his grownups the truth, and together, they decided how to keep Jimmy safe.

What Jimmy and his grownups couldn't have known >>>>>>>>>>>>>>>>>>>

>>>>>>> was that Adam was a grownup pretending to be a kid, and that he planned to use those pictures to embarrass Jimmy.

This is an example of why

ONLINE SAFETY

MATTERS.

BEING SAFE ONLINE MEANS KNOWING WHO YOU'RE TALKING TO AND BEING CAREFUL ABOUT WHAT YOU SHARE WITH OTHERS.

Not everyone you talk to online is a nice person.

And believe it or not, both kids and grownups can be tricked by folks online.

And when it happens, kids can:

BE BULLIED,

GET HURT EMOTIONALLY,

OR BE PUT IN PHYSICAL DANGER.

And this can leave them feeling:

SCARED,

UNSAFE,

AND ALL ALONE.

WE KNOW THIS IS
A LOT TO THINK ABOUT.

As easy as it is to be online,
sometimes the consequences
can be pretty harsh.

And online interactions
can hurt you in real life, too.

But we want you to
know something...

YOU ARE NOT

ALONE.

And if something happens,
it's not your fault.

There are lots of ways
to stay safe online.

HERE ARE SOME
THINGS YOU CAN DO:

ALWAYS
STOP
AND
THINK.

Don't rush to make decisions online, especially if someone else really wants you to hurry.

Think about what you're doing, ask questions, and trust your instincts.

Know it is **ALWAYS** OK to say no.

DON'T
SHARE
PERSONAL
INFORMATION.

You never need to share things like pictures or videos of yourself (especially your private body parts), phone numbers, passwords, or anything like that with someone online.

Once you share something, who sees it next is totally out of your control.

Use the privacy settings in your apps, games, and on your device to keep from sharing accidentally.

DON'T
BELIEVE
EVERYTHING
ONLINE.

Be aware of the websites and apps you visit, and what people online tell you about themselves.

There are a lot of untrue things on the Internet that can be harmful.

And most importantly...

DON'T
BE AFRAID
TO TELL
A TRUSTED
GROWNUP.

You can **always** talk to a trusted grownup like a parent, teacher, aunt, uncle, librarian, or coach.

No matter what.

As specialists who work in this space, we know what we're talking about.

And here are a few important things to remember:

Just because it's online, doesn't mean it doesn't matter.

Not everyone online is safe for you.

What goes online stays around forever._

The Internet can be a
dangerous place,

but it is also an amazing place, filled with good information, fun activities, and useful programs.

And now, you have helpful tools
to make it a safer space for

YOU AND YOU

JR FRIENDS.

Outro
for grownups

Thank you for opening this important conversation with the kids in your life. We hope the discussion about online safety and what you can do to stay safe while using the Internet doesn't stop here.

Keep an open, honest dialogue going about what your kids are experiencing in their online world. Maybe run through some role-playing examples, like our story about Jimmy and his grownups. Go through the questions we've included below and chat about your answers.

Remember that making smart choices can help keep you and your loved ones safe online *and* offline.

1. Is there anything that keeps you from talking with a grownup about what happens online?

2. Are there things in the past that have made you feel weird, or you have questions about?

3. What are the things you already do today that keep you safe online?

4. After reading this book, is there anything that you'd like to change to be more safe online?

About The Authors

We are a group of security and cybersecurity professionals dedicated to making the Internet a safer place for kids and grownups alike!

Notable contributors to this book are Vivian Choy, Harold Chun, Shiao Lee, Lorrie Ma, Katie Martin, Henry Person, Albert Shin, and Erin Thackston Thon.

Made to empower.

Discover more at akidsco.com